MUSIC MONEY

TURNING PASSION INTO PROFITS FOR DADS!!

Music Money

Turning Passion into Profits for Dads!!

Contents

Introduction

Welcome to *"Music Money: Turning Passion into Profits for Dads!!"* If you're a dad with a deep passion for music, this guide is tailored just for you!

Whether you're a guitar-strumming aficionado, a piano-playing maestro, or just someone who loves music and has always wanted to have a career doing something that involves music, you're about to embark on a journey that could not only amplify your skills but also pad your wallet!

In today's fast-paced world, where pursuing your passion can often seem like a luxury, it's remarkable how many dads are taking their musical talents and leveraging them to create extra income. According to a recent survey conducted by the Music Industry Research Association, over 35% of adults who engage in music-related hobbies express a desire to monetize those talents.

Nowadays, the intersection of passion and profit is an exciting avenue that's more accessible than ever before! Imagine strumming your guitar to a live audience and getting paid for it, or visualize sharing your musical insights with a global community through online tutorials and receiving a steady stream of income. These dreams are within reach, and this guide will equip you with the knowledge and strategies to make them a reality.

Statistics show that the online music education market has witnessed a staggering 50% growth in the last five years, with no signs of slowing down. As a dad, you're in a unique position to tap into this trend!

Not only can you bring your musical expertise to the table, but you can also impart your skills to aspiring musicians, creating a positive impact while adding to your earnings.

While pursuing a career in the music industry may have seemed daunting in the past, the digital age has democratized the playing field. Through the power of social media and online platforms, artists are now capable of reaching a global audience with just a few clicks.

According to the Global Music Report, independent musicians experienced a 32% increase in streaming revenue last year alone, highlighting the potential for growth in the independent music sector.

However, it's essential to remember that while the opportunities are abundant, success won't be handed to you on a silver platter. This journey will require dedication, continuous learning, and adaptability. From determining your niche to building your website, each step comes with its own set of challenges and rewards.

In this guide, we'll explore various ways you can transform your musical passion into a thriving source of income. From teaching music lessons and creating online courses to performing live and delving into the world of music production, you'll find a range of strategies that suit your unique skills and preferences.

The chapters that follow will dive into each monetization opportunity, providing practical advice, case studies, and actionable steps to help you navigate the path to success. Remember, you're not just monetizing your music – you're sharing your passion with the world while securing a stable financial future for yourself and your family!

Also, if at any time you decide, "I'm ready to move forward!" at the end of each chapter is a link to the masterclass that got me started on my own entrepreneurial journey and the program I recommend to everyone!

So, whether you're a seasoned musician looking to diversify your income or a music-loving dad who's ready to take the plunge, this guide is your compass to charting a course toward both artistic fulfillment and financial prosperity. Get ready to harmonize your passion with profit and make your musical dreams resonate in ways you never thought possible!

Ready to turn your passion into reality?
Follow the link and begin your journey!

www.rock-dads.com/successpath

Chapter 1:

Teaching and Sharing Your Expertise

Unlocking Earnings Through Music Education

If you've ever felt the rush of joy that comes from playing a musical instrument or singing your heart out, imagine sharing that feeling with others while also earning an income.

Recent studies show that the demand for music education is on the rise. In fact, the National Association for Music Education reports that nearly 60% of parents believe music education is essential for their child's development. This presents an exciting opportunity for dads who are passionate about music to step into the role of a music educator.

Why Teach Music?

Teaching music not only allows you to pass on your skills but also fosters a strong connection with your community. Research indicates that students who receive musical education tend to have improved cognitive abilities, better academic performance, and enhanced self-confidence.

Private Lessons and Online Teaching

One popular way to teach music is by offering private lessons. These can take place in your own home or through online platforms. According to a study by the Music Teachers National Association, over 70% of music teachers offer online lessons, and this number is expected to grow. This flexible approach caters to busy schedules and allows you to reach students from all over the world.

Also, the online barrier to entry is fairly low when all you need is a computer or mobile device, a virtual room like Zoom or MSFT Teams, and a way to generate leads to get started. Plus, there's always the option of doing both!!

Creating Engaging Lesson Plans

Crafting engaging lesson plans is key to keeping your students motivated and eager to learn. Break down complex concepts into manageable steps, and incorporate fun activities that align with your students' interests. Remember, a great teacher not only imparts knowledge but also ignites a lifelong love for music!

These lesson plans can make great lead magnets and can drive people to your site or appointment scheduler when given away for free. By creating a fun and interesting first lesson, you can hook the audience to engage (and pay for) the rest of your course!

Building a Reputation

When teaching music, your reputation is your strongest asset. Positive word-of-mouth from satisfied students and parents can go a long way. Showcase your expertise through your teaching methods, performance achievements, and testimonials. Utilize social media and local community groups to spread the word about your music lessons.

This might seem difficult to do at first, but the reality is we often make things more complicated than they need to be. It would be easy to say, "How can I build a reputation when I've never had clients who can vouch for my methodology?". That's a valid concern; however, there are other ways to build a reputation. Creating and posting tips and tricks on social media and then using those comments as reviews can be a great way to spread the word about how your teaching method is valid and worth further exploration!

Diversifying Income: Workshops and Masterclasses

While one-on-one lessons are a staple, consider diversifying your income by offering workshops and masterclasses. These focused sessions can cover specific techniques, genres, or even music theory. They attract both beginners and more advanced learners, adding variety to your teaching portfolio.

This also provides an opportunity for an offer stack. Essentially, it gives you more opportunities for your consumers to engage with you! For example, you could teach guitar basics as one offer, then offer an advanced class, and then offer separate classes specific to music genres that you enjoy playing!

Embracing the Journey

Teaching music is not just about transferring technical skills – it's about inspiring creativity, fostering discipline, and nurturing a passion for music in others. The fulfillment that comes from witnessing your students' progress is immeasurable in the same way it is when you are teaching your own kids!

In summary, in this digital age, teaching music has become more accessible and rewarding than ever. Online platforms provide the tools you need to create engaging lessons, connect with students globally, and generate income. As you embark on your journey as a music educator, remember that you're not just teaching notes; you're imparting the gift of music to the next generation while building a solid foundation for your own financial success!

Ready to turn your passion into reality?
Follow the link and begin your journey!

www.rock-dads.com/successpath

Chapter 2:

Creating a Digital Presence

Amplifying Your Musical Impact Online

The internet has transformed how we connect and share. Having a strong digital presence is essential for any dad looking to monetize his musical passion. This chapter dives into creating an impactful online presence and how it can turn your love for music into a thriving income source.

The Power of Going Digital

Did you know that over 4.9 billion people around the world use the Internet? That's more than half of the global population! Harnessing the internet's reach can help you connect with a massive audience, whether they're next door or halfway across the world. Your online presence can extend your musical influence far beyond what was possible just a few years ago.

Crafting Your Online Identity

Before diving into the digital world, it's crucial to establish a clear and authentic online identity. This starts with creating a compelling website or blog that showcases your musical journey, expertise, and offerings. According to a survey by HubSpot, companies with blogs generate 55%

more website visits, indicating the importance of consistent online content.

If you are not technically inclined, this may seem a bit daunting. It is actually a lot easier than you think. You would buy an available domain, build your website (or have someone else do it! Fiverr is a great place to get low-cost help!), then run ads or leads to the website. As long as you have a way of getting the customer's information with a pop-up, form, or scheduler, you're in business!

Leveraging Social Media

Social media platforms like Facebook, Instagram, and TikTok offer powerful tools to connect with fans and potential students. Statistics show that musicians and artists are among the top content categories on platforms like Instagram, making it a prime space to showcase your musical talent. Engage with your audience through regular posts, videos, and live sessions to create a loyal online following.

In the beginning, don't get too caught up in overall production quality. Focus on the most immediate and important thing—consistency, consistency, consistency!

Whether you plan out and schedule your content or just want to wing it, make sure that you are consistent in getting your content in front of people!

YouTube as a Content Hub

YouTube, with over 2 billion logged-in monthly users, is a treasure trove for musicians. It's not just a platform for sharing music videos; it's also a place to upload tutorials, covers, vlogs, and original compositions. The more valuable content you share, the more likely you are to attract subscribers and views, which can translate to ad revenue and sponsorships.

This is also part of your business ecosystem. You can use your website to reference your YouTube site and vice versa, which keeps people engaged with your brand!

Podcasting for a Personal Touch

The popularity of podcasts is on the rise, and it's a fantastic way for dads to share their musical insights and experiences. According to Edison Research, 104 million Americans are monthly podcast listeners. Hosting a music-related podcast can help you connect with an engaged audience and even open up sponsorship opportunities.

Podcasts are fun, but income, in most cases, takes a lot of time. That is not to scare anyone away from doing it. The most valuable commodity you have is time, and podcasts take up A LOT of time. If you feel like you have the time and can be consistent with curating a podcast, by all means, do it!! Rock Dads recommends that you establish your business before diving into podcasting full-time.

Digital Marketing Strategies

When it comes to your online presence, quality content is king, but effective digital marketing is the queen that makes it all work. Utilize strategies like search engine optimization (SEO), email marketing, and paid advertising to ensure that your content reaches the right people at the right time.

Like learning an instrument, these are skills that you develop. And unlike the saying, you can teach an old dog new tricks! Once you have an understanding of how these things relate to one another and how they translate to engaging your audience, you'll be a marketing pro in no time!

The Global Stage

The beauty of the internet is that it doesn't limit your reach. Whether you're in a small town or a bustling city, your music can resonate across the globe. Sharing your passion online can lead to collaboration opportunities, paid gigs, and even students enrolling in your online courses from different continents!

In conclusion, attention spans are shrinking, and competition is fierce; therefore, creating a robust digital presence is more important than ever. By crafting an authentic online identity, utilizing social media platforms, and leveraging tools like YouTube and podcasts, you can amplify your musical impact and tap into an audience eager to support your journey. As a dad with a passion for music, embracing the digital realm can not only elevate your musical career but also open up a world of financial opportunities!

Ready to turn your passion into reality?

Follow the link and begin your journey!

www.rock-dads.com/successpath

Chapter 3:

Crafting Online Courses

Transforming Musical Expertise into Lucrative

Learning Experiences

If you're a dad with a wealth of musical knowledge and a desire to share it, creating online courses could be your ticket to turning your passion into profit. In this chapter, we'll explore online education and how you can leverage your expertise to generate income while making a lasting impact.

The Boom in Online Learning

The e-learning industry has been on an upward trajectory, and recent data reveals that the global e-learning market is expected to reach $325 billion by 2025. This trend opens up an incredible avenue for dads to teach music to a diverse and eager audience.

Identifying Your Niche

Before diving into course creation, consider your unique strengths and musical expertise. Are you a whiz at jazz piano improvisation? Do you have a knack for teaching vocal harmonies? Identifying your niche will help you create focused, valuable courses that cater to a specific audience.

Many times, that specific audience is you...or at least someone similar to you. That is why it is incredibly important to spend an adequate amount of time on your story and your brand so that it resonates with the audience.

Choosing the Right Platform

Selecting the right online course platform is a pivotal decision. Platforms like Udemy, Teachable, and Coursera offer user-friendly tools for creating and marketing your courses. Research conducted by Statista indicates that over 50% of learners prefer video-based content in online courses, underscoring the importance of a visual and engaging learning experience.

Designing Engaging Curriculum

Creating an effective online course involves more than just sharing your musical wisdom. It's about structuring your content in a way that keeps learners engaged and motivated. Break down complex concepts into digestible modules, incorporate quizzes and assignments, and provide practical exercises to reinforce learning.

Curriculum building can take a considerable amount of time, but it is the product you are selling. Take time to recall how you learned, research other online instructors, and subscribe to their newsletters to get an idea of how they are designing workflows for their audience and how you might do the same!

Promoting Your Courses

Even the best courses won't succeed without effective marketing. Utilize social media, your website, and even partnerships with other musicians to spread the word about your courses. Remember, a well-crafted landing page that highlights the benefits and outcomes of your course can significantly impact enrollment rates.

Patience and adaptability are critical here. At the start of promoting your business, give your ads time to generate analytics before you begin adjusting things. At the same time, it is important to review those analytics and make the necessary adjustments to maximize your ad investments. You can't just play music and make videos all day...you're an entrepreneur now!!

Creating Value Through Interaction

One of the advantages of online courses is the opportunity for interaction. Host live Q&A sessions, discussion forums, and personalized feedback sessions to foster a sense of community among your students. Research shows that courses with active community elements tend to have higher completion rates.

Monetizing Your Expertise

When it comes to monetization, online courses offer various revenue streams. You can opt for one-time course purchases, monthly subscriptions, or even bundle multiple courses for a premium offering. As mentioned before, with offer stacking, there are many ways to introduce your courses and upsell your clients that are seamless and appropriate for your audience.

A Legacy of Learning

Creating online courses isn't just about financial gain;

it's about leaving a legacy of knowledge. By sharing your musical expertise with a global audience, you're contributing to the growth of aspiring musicians and music enthusiasts worldwide.

In conclusion, your unique perspective and expertise can stand out and make a meaningful impact. By crafting engaging courses, choosing the right platform, and marketing effectively, you can transform your love for music into a profitable venture that empowers learners while adding to your income.

So, whether you're teaching guitar chords or unraveling the mysteries of music theory, the world of online courses awaits your transformative journey!

Ready to turn your passion into reality?
Follow the link and begin your journey!

www.rock-dads.com/successpath

Chapter 4:

The Art of Music Production

Turning Your Musical Creativity into Marketable Tracks

Behind every great song is a skilled music producer who transforms ideas into sonic masterpieces. If you're a dad with a knack for arranging, recording, and mixing, this chapter explores how you can monetize your musical talents through the art of music production.

The Rise of Independent Music Production

The music industry landscape has shifted, with independent artists and producers gaining more prominence. According to a report by MIDiA Research, independent musicians accounted for 39% of the global recorded music market in 2020. This presents a golden opportunity for dads with a passion for music production to collaborate with emerging artists and established acts alike.

Crafting Captivating Productions

As a music producer, your role goes beyond pressing buttons and twiddling knobs. It's about translating an artist's vision into a polished and captivating sound. Understanding different genres, experimenting with sound effects, and refining your mixing skills can set you apart in the competitive world of music production.

If music production is an area you don't have much skill in but want to develop, there are some great schools out there that can give you hands-on, real-world education without breaking the bank. Full Sail Academy and SAE Institute are great options!

Building a Portfolio

Just like a musician needs a repertoire of songs, a music producer needs a portfolio of work to showcase their skills. Collaborate with local artists, offer your services for free initially to build relationships, and gradually expand your network. A strong portfolio can open doors to paid projects and collaborations with diverse talents.

You can also take your portfolio and upload it to websites that allow users to buy your songs! Just because you give it away on one platform doesn't mean you can't sell it on another!

Navigating the Digital Audio Workstation (DAW)

A key tool for any music producer is the Digital Audio Workstation or DAW. Platforms like Ableton Live, Logic Pro, and Pro Tools empower you to create, edit, and manipulate audio.

Some of these options may be pricey for where you are in your journey, but it is imperative that you know how to navigate DAWs if you are going to assist artists in music production or produce your own music. If needs be, start out with free or inexpensive DAWs, like Audacity, to begin cutting your teeth and developing your skills.

Offering Mixing and Mastering Services

One of the crucial stages in music production is mixing and mastering, where the raw tracks are refined into a polished final product. If you excel at this process, you can offer your services to artists looking to enhance their tracks' quality. The rise of streaming platforms and the need for professional-sounding tracks further accentuates the demand for skilled mixers and masters.

Marketing Your Production Skills

Effective marketing can make the difference between being a sought-after producer and being one of many. Showcase your portfolio on your website, social media platforms, and relevant online forums. Engage with artists and music communities to demonstrate your expertise and build your reputation.

You may have to go out of your comfort zone when reaching out to people. If you have built up a body of work and have taken the time to do your own promoting and website development, you have a solid foundation to show your professionalism, passion, and expertise.

Monetizing Through Royalties and Fees

As a music producer, your income can come from various sources. You can charge a flat fee for your services, negotiate royalties from song sales and streaming, and even consider offering production packages for artists. According to the Music Producers Guild, producers often receive royalties ranging from 3% to 5% of an artist's record sales.

From Passion to Paycheck

Music production is a fusion of technical expertise and artistic creativity. By turning your love for creating music into a profitable venture, you're not only enhancing your own skills but also playing a pivotal role in shaping the sonic landscape of the music industry!

In summary, as you embark on your journey as a music producer, remember that each project you undertake contributes to your growth and reputation. Whether you're working with indie artists or established names, your role in shaping their sound is integral. The art of music production allows you to monetize your passion while weaving your musical magic into tracks that resonate with audiences worldwide!

Ready to turn your passion into reality?
Follow the link and begin your journey!

www.rock-dads.com/successpath

Chapter 5:

Songwriting and Composition

Transforming Melodies and Lyrics into Lucrative Art

If you've ever found yourself lost in the world of melodies and lyrics, this chapter offers a pathway to turning your songwriting passion into a source of income. As a dad with a gift for crafting captivating tunes, this chapter explores how you can monetize your songwriting and composition skills.

The Demand for Original Music

In a digital age where content is king, the demand for original music has never been higher. According to the International Federation of the Phonographic Industry, streaming revenue from recorded music saw a 19.9% increase in 2020. This underscores the need for fresh, engaging music, making it an opportune time for songwriters to shine.

Also, take into consideration where people are learning about and consuming music. Social media platforms are rife with new artists and new opportunities. You could have the next viral TikTok tune, and it could be just 5 seconds long!!

Crafting Memorable Melodies and Lyrics

As a songwriter, your ability to tell stories through music is invaluable. Crafting melodies that resonate with emotions and lyrics that capture the human experience can set your songs apart. Study the works of celebrated songwriters and analyze the elements that make their compositions compelling.

Exploring Different Genres and Styles

Diversity is the spice of songwriting. While you might have a preferred genre, exploring different styles can expand your creative palette. According to a survey by Nielsen, nearly 50% of music listeners reported enjoying a variety of music genres, indicating the potential audience for your compositions.

Plus…it's fun!!

Collaborating with Artists

Collaboration is at the heart of the music industry. Join forces with singers and bands to transform your compositions into fully-fledged songs. Your melodies and lyrics, combined with their vocal prowess, can create a musical synergy that resonates with audiences.

And if you're not ready to ask Axl Rose or Mick Jagger to collaborate on your next great tune, start with local artists. Many, as you are probably already well aware, are looking to create as much as they can and broaden their audience as well. Who knows if you and someone who lives down the street from you are going to be the next Eminem and Dr. Dre or Korn and Ross Robinson!

Licensing Your Music

Licensing your original music for various media is a lucrative avenue. Films, TV shows, commercials, and video games constantly seek unique tracks to enhance their content. According to the Music Publishers Association, synchronization royalties for music used in media can generate substantial income for songwriters.

You could go directly to ASCAP or BMI to start licensing your music. Depending on how serious you want to get, you could also hire a licensing attorney to help navigate the legalities and lean on their connections in the greater music business.

Navigating Copyright and Publishing

Protecting your intellectual property is crucial. Understand copyright laws and consider registering your compositions with a Performing Rights Organization (PRO) to ensure you receive royalties for public performances. The Global Music Report indicates that performance royalties accounted for 38% of total music industry revenue in 2020. Don't miss out on your share because you don't know the law!

Promoting Your Catalog

A well-curated catalog of original compositions can serve as your musical portfolio. Create a professional website or platform to showcase your songs, making it easier for potential collaborators, artists, and media creators to discover and license your work.

Honestly, this should be a no-brainer by now. You need a place where you can curate and direct anyone and everyone to experience your music. The easiest might be a YouTube channel, but if you want a more personal touch, Rock Dads recommends a stand-alone website.

Monetizing Through Royalties and Licensing

One of the primary ways songwriters earn income is through royalties. Performance royalties, mechanical royalties from sales and streaming, and synchronization royalties from media placements contribute to your earnings. A study by Berklee College of Music found that sync placements can earn songwriters between $500 and $45,000 per placement.

This is another reason why it may benefit you to hire a lawyer. These laws can be tricky, and you know corporations that want to solicit your music have lawyers protecting their interests as well.

Melodies That Pay

Songwriting isn't just an art; it's a business opportunity. By combining your passion for melodies and lyrics with a strategic approach to monetization, you're crafting a pathway to earn from what you love most!

To sum up, as you embark on your journey as a songwriter and composer, remember that each song you create carries the potential to resonate with listeners across the globe. Whether you're writing for yourself, collaborating with artists, or licensing your music for media, your compositions have the power to evoke emotions, tell stories, and contribute to your financial success!

Ready to turn your passion into reality?
Follow the link and begin your journey!

www.rock-dads.com/successpath

Chapter 6:

Performance Opportunities

Taking the Stage and Turning Passion into Paycheck

For the dad with a burning desire to share their musical talents with a live audience, this chapter unveils the world of live performances and how it can be a fulfilling opportunity to monetize your musical passion!

The Thrill of Live Performances

There's an electrifying magic that happens when you step onto a stage and connect with an audience through your music. The allure of live performances remains strong; according to a survey by Statista, over 52% of adults in the United States attend live music events each year. This presents a remarkable opportunity for dads to captivate audiences while generating income.

From Local Gigs to Global Reach

Live performances encompass a range of opportunities, from local venues to international festivals. Even if you're starting small, local gigs provide a platform to showcase your talent and build a fanbase. The rise of social media allows you to extend your reach beyond geographical boundaries, attracting listeners from around the world.

There is incredible room for fast growth and exposure here if you maximize each opportunity. Getting video of any and every time you play, no matter where is content that can go on your website and social media platforms; it's a record of past live performances that can provide leverage for future performances, and you can hone your act when you watch yourself perform from the audience's perspective!

Selling Tickets and Merchandise

Whether you're performing at a small club or a larger concert hall, selling tickets is a primary revenue stream. According to Pollstar, concert ticket sales generated over $12 billion in revenue globally in 2019. Additionally, merchandise sales can significantly boost your earnings. Branded T-shirts, posters, and even exclusive music releases create a memorable connection with your fans.

You do NOT have to be a design expert to add merchandise to your offer stack. Hire someone to create a design you approve of, take that design to Printify, Printful, or some other similar site, choose the apparel you want to sell, apply the design, and order however many you want to sell. There might be some upfront cost, but as long as you are selling over what you paid for them, you're making money!

Crafting an Unforgettable Set

Creating an engaging live performance involves more than just playing your songs; it's about curating an experience that resonates with your audience. Mix up your setlist with familiar tunes and original compositions. Interact with the audience and share personal stories that provide insight into your music.

Go see other local artists to see how they do it, what songs they are playing, what the audience is getting into, etc. Be a student of the art of the show!

Weddings, Parties, and Special Events

Beyond traditional music venues, there's a demand for live music at weddings, parties, and special events. The Knot's 2020 Real Weddings Study reported that couples allocated an average of $2,000 for live music at their weddings. This presents an opportunity for dads to offer their musical talents for unforgettable moments.

The great thing about these types of occasions is that most of the time, the songs are picked for you or are obvious ones you need to learn in order to play the gig. This can be a steady source of income and give you time to work on your original stuff.

Virtual Concerts and Livestreams

The digital age has opened up new avenues for live performances. Virtual concerts and livestreams allow you to connect with a global audience from the comfort of your home. A study by Bandsintown revealed that 27% of artists performed virtual shows in 2020, showcasing the increasing prevalence of this trend.

An argument can be made that the increase was due to COVID-19, and musicians were doing whatever they could to get their music out. It doesn't discount that after the pandemic subsided, artists continued to do these virtual shows as another creative outlet.

Marketing and Promotion

Effectively marketing your live performances is

essential for drawing in audiences. Utilize social media platforms, email marketing, and partnerships with local venues to spread the word. Engage with your fans through behind-the-scenes content and updates about upcoming shows.

If you've built up a following on your social platforms, it's relatively easy and inexpensive to spread the word about any upcoming shows you may have. That being said, don't let the venue forget to promote your show and get it in the local paper's print copy and online events sections!

Monetizing Through Performance Fees and Merchandise Sales

Your income from live performances comes primarily from performance fees and merchandise sales. Negotiating fair fees for your performances, combined with strategic pricing for your merchandise, can help you maximize your earnings. A study by the Musicians' Union found that the average fee for a live performance in the UK ranged from £75 to £400. That's $92 to $489 in the US, and don't forget, that's without merchandising sales.

Harmonizing Passion and Profit

Live performances allow you to share your musical talents while also reaping financial rewards. Each stage you step onto provides an opportunity to not only connect with fans but also create lasting memories for both yourself and your audience.

In conclusion, as you set out on your path as a live entertainer, keep in mind that the stage serves as your canvas, and your music acts as the brushstroke that illustrates feelings, recollections, and tunes. Whether you're delivering your performance in cozy venues or on grander platforms, the realm of live music encourages you to blend your zeal and financial gains in manners that have the potential to reshape your musical voyage!

Ready to turn your passion into reality?
Follow the link and begin your journey!

www.rock-dads.com/successpath

Chapter 7:

Diversifying Income Streams

Expanding Your Musical Horizons for Maximum Earnings

For the dad looking to amplify their musical earnings, this chapter is a treasure trove of strategies to diversify income streams. Embracing multiple avenues of revenue can turn your passion for music into a resilient and thriving financial venture. We've covered some of these, but it's helpful to have things in one place to give another perspective on how they can work together.

Why Diversify?

As the saying goes, don't put all your eggs in one basket. This rings true for monetizing your musical passion as well. According to a survey by the Freelancers Union, 70% of freelancers diversify their income sources to safeguard against economic uncertainties. Diversification not only increases your earning potential but also creates stability in an ever-changing music industry.

Merchandise: Beyond Music

Branded merchandise offers a tangible way for fans to connect with your musical brand. Whether it's T-shirts, stickers, or even limited edition items, selling merchandise can add a significant revenue stream. The Recording Industry Association of America reported that merchandising sales increased by 18% in 2020.

It's never been easier to develop and curate a merchandising line. A simple Shopify store can be the place you send people online, and you can pre-print what you need for shows. There's very little need for warehousing, and you can even make designs specific to shows that aren't available on the website to make your merchandise even more exclusive!

Crowdfunding and Patronage

Platforms like Patreon and Kickstarter allow you to gather support from dedicated fans who believe in your music. Offering exclusive content, early releases, and personalized interactions can incentivize fans to become patrons. According to Patreon, creators on their platform earned over $2 billion from patrons by 2020.

Music Licensing and Sync Placements

Licensing your music for various media projects can be a lucrative avenue. Films, TV shows, commercials, and video games are always on the lookout for original tracks. The global sync licensing market is projected to reach $1.8 billion by 2025, offering a significant opportunity for songwriters and composers.

Collaborations and Featured Appearances

Teaming up with other artists and musicians can expand your reach and introduce your music to new audiences. Whether it's guest appearances on tracks, cross-promotions, or collaborative projects, collaborations can lead to increased visibility and earnings.

Online Workshops and Masterclasses

Your musical expertise can be shared beyond individual lessons. Hosting online workshops and masterclasses allows you to cater to a larger audience while offering in-depth insights. The global e-learning market is expected to continue its growth, presenting a prime opportunity for dads to monetize their teaching skills.

Affiliate Marketing and Partnerships

If you use and love certain musical products, consider affiliate marketing. Promote instruments, software, or equipment you endorse, and earn a commission on sales generated through your unique links. According to a survey by Rakuten Advertising, 80% of consumers trust online reviews as much as personal recommendations.

This is SUPER easy if you already have a website or platform on which you can promote the product or service. You get a link from the manufacturer or site that you want to promote, and then you share that link with your audience...pretty simple. There are various ways you can advertise the link. That's a completely different book!!

Creating Sample Packs and Sound Libraries

For dads with a knack for sound design and music production, creating sample packs and sound libraries can be profitable. Music producers and creators are always on the lookout for high-quality sounds to use in their projects.

Balancing Passion and Profit

Diversifying your income streams isn't just about making money; it's about building a resilient musical career. By embracing multiple avenues of revenue, you're ensuring that your passion for music remains a sustainable and fulfilling endeavor. Keep in mind, however, that Rock Dads does not recommend you try all of these opportunities at once. It's important to start with a foundation in one or two areas, get them to a sustainable place, and then begin exploring diversification.

In summary, as you embark on the journey of diversifying your musical income, remember that each new avenue you explore adds to your expertise and contributes to your financial growth. Whether you're selling merchandise, collaborating with other artists, or licensing your music, the world of diversification invites you to orchestrate a symphony of success that resonates with both your musical aspirations and your financial goals!

Ready to turn your passion into reality?
Follow the link and begin your journey!

www.rock-dads.com/successpath

Chapter 8:

Music and Wellness

Harmonizing Music and Well-being for Impactful Earnings

For the dad who understands the healing power of music, this chapter delves into the world of music and wellness, revealing how you can use your musical talents to positively impact people's emotional and psychological well-being while generating income.

The Healing Notes of Music

Research has shown that music has therapeutic effects on individuals' mental and emotional states. A study published in the Journal of Music Therapy found that music therapy can reduce symptoms of depression and anxiety. As a dad, your musical talents can be a source of solace for those seeking emotional well-being.

The Role of Music Therapy

Music therapy is a recognized field that utilizes music to address emotional, cognitive, and social needs. According to the American Music Therapy Association, music therapists use techniques such as playing instruments, singing, and composing to improve mental health. Your proficiency in music positions you to offer therapeutic sessions that can positively impact lives.

Creating Therapeutic Music Sessions

Crafting therapeutic music sessions involves creating an environment where individuals can relax, express themselves, and experience emotional release through music. Tailor your sessions to different needs, whether it's relaxation, stress reduction, or emotional exploration.

These curated songscapes can also be packaged and sold, creating more opportunities for your music to earn money!

Wellness Workshops and Retreats

Host wellness workshops and retreats that integrate music and mindfulness techniques. A study by the Global Wellness Institute revealed that the wellness industry was valued at $4.5 trillion in 2018. By offering unique experiences that combine music, relaxation, and self-care, you can tap into this growing market.

If you aren't too familiar with the wellness side of things, partner with someone who is! They may be excited at the prospect of using local artists' music for their clients!

Music for Stress Reduction

Stress is a pervasive issue, with the American Psychological Association reporting that 75% of adults experience moderate to high levels of stress. Your soothing melodies and calming compositions can provide a refuge for individuals seeking respite from the pressures of daily life.

As mentioned above, you can collaborate with other business owners to use your music or sell it online! And not just in your own store, you can place it anywhere similar products are sold or wherever you choose to promote it: Pinterest, Etsy, etc.!

Collaborating with Therapists and Professionals

Collaboration with mental health professionals and therapists can add depth to your offerings. By integrating your musical expertise with therapeutic techniques, you can create comprehensive programs that address a range of emotional needs.

Online Sessions and Digital Offerings

The digital landscape allows you to reach a wider audience through online music therapy sessions and resources. The growth of telehealth services has expanded opportunities for remote therapy sessions, enabling you to connect with clients globally.

Monetizing Through Music and Wellness Services

Monetizing your music and wellness services involves offering packages, workshops, and sessions at competitive rates. According to a survey by the American Music Therapy Association, the average hourly rate for board-certified music therapists ranged from $60 to $100.

Today, there are over 9,000 board-certified music therapists in the US. If you are interested in becoming a board-certified music therapist, you'll need a degree and state licensing. Be sure to review your state's requirements before going into business!

A Harmonious Blend of Passion and Impact

The fusion of music and wellness is a space where your musical passion can be a catalyst for transformation and healing. By creating sessions that resonate with individuals seeking emotional well-being, you're not only enriching their lives but also creating a meaningful source of income for yourself.

Remember, your ability to create an atmosphere of healing through music is a gift. Whether you're offering therapeutic sessions, wellness workshops, or digital resources, your music has the potential to touch hearts and souls while contributing to your financial future!

Ready to turn your passion into reality?
Follow the link and begin your journey!

www.rock-dads.com/successpath

Chapter 9:

Music and Technology

Innovative Ways to Fuse Music and Tech for Profits

For the tech-savvy dad with a passion for music, this chapter unveils the dynamic intersection of music and technology. Discover how you can leverage cutting-edge tools and platforms to not only enhance your musical creations but also generate income in innovative ways.

The Digital Evolution of Music

The music industry has undergone a digital revolution, with technology shaping how music is created, distributed, and consumed. According to the Recording Industry Association of America, streaming music revenue accounted for 83% of the total industry revenue in 2020. This digital landscape presents a wealth of opportunities for dads to blend their musical talents with tech innovations!

Music Production Software and DAWs

Digital Audio Workstations (DAWs) and music production software have revolutionized how music is created. Platforms like Ableton Live and Logic Pro enable musicians to compose, arrange, and produce intricate tracks with ease.

Embrace these tools to create professional-quality music from the comfort of your home studio.

If you are well-versed in how these systems operate, you can either offer those services or offer to TEACH how they operate to those who may be trying to get into music production. You could offer online courses or one-on-one guidance!

Virtual Instruments and Sound Libraries

Virtual instruments have expanded the sonic palette available to musicians. From realistic piano and orchestral sounds to exotic instruments, these virtual tools allow you to create diverse compositions. According to a report by Technavio, the virtual instruments market is expected to grow by $221.2 million during 2021-2025.

Musicians are always looking for new sounds and sound augmentation technology to create unique styles that can set them apart. Collaborating with musicians on what sounds they would like to make or providing a few for them to test can help you build products that you can promote under your brand!!

Music for Media and Gaming

The gaming and media industries offer promising avenues for music monetization. Video games, podcasts, and online videos constantly seek captivating music to enhance the user experience. A study by SuperData Research estimated that the global gaming industry generated $139.9 billion in revenue in 2020, presenting a substantial market for musicians.

As soon as we start talking about licensing, we have to talk about lawyers. These outlets are incredibly far-reaching and can get your music in front of thousands, if not millions of people. That's why it is so incredibly important to make sure you are protected.

Creating Music for Apps and Software

With the surge in mobile app usage, developers seek original music to enhance their apps' appeal. Whether it's calming background music or energetic tunes, your compositions can become an integral part of users' experiences. The app economy is projected to be valued at $6.3 trillion by 2021, highlighting the demand for engaging app content.

As we've stated before, getting your music on places like Instagram and TikTok, predominantly app-centered platforms, can be a great way to reach a massive audience that can then experience your music via your social or website platforms.

Digital Distribution and Streaming Platforms

Digital distribution has democratized music publishing. Platforms like Spotify, Apple Music, and Amazon Music allow independent musicians to share their music with a global audience. A study by Statista found that the revenue from streaming music subscriptions exceeded $20 billion in 2020.

Each of these platforms has their own rules. Make sure you know them before submitting your music to avoid complications and/or lawsuits.

Blockchain and Music Royalties

Blockchain technology has the potential to revolutionize how musicians are paid for their work. By creating a transparent and decentralized system, artists can receive fair compensation for their music. A report by MarketsandMarkets projected that the blockchain market for the music industry could reach $1.64 billion by 2023.

This is still a fairly new idea in its application to music and artists. However, it has tremendous potential to bridge the gap between artists and their audiences when it comes to fair compensation for their art.

Monetizing Music Tech Solutions

You can monetize your tech-savvy skills by offering music tech solutions to fellow musicians. This could include creating custom sound libraries, developing plugins, or providing technical support. According to a survey by Digital Music News, over 58% of musicians use plugins for music production.

While fellow musicians may be the warmest market, there are still plenty of people out there looking to improve their skills in what you may already be an expert in. Experiment with different audiences to see if you can't expand your potential clientele and thus increase your profits!

The Symphony of Music and Tech

The fusion of music and technology isn't just a trend; it's a transformative force that can shape the future of your musical journey. By embracing innovative tools, platforms, and approaches, you're not only enhancing your creative capabilities but also positioning yourself to profit in a rapidly evolving industry.

In conclusion, as you navigate the realm of music and technology, remember that each innovation you adopt expands your potential to create, collaborate, and captivate audiences. Whether you're composing for virtual reality experiences, designing app soundtracks, or revolutionizing music distribution, the world of music and tech invites you to compose a symphony of profits that harmonizes your passion and expertise!

Ready to turn your passion into reality?

Follow the link and begin your journey!

www.rock-dads.com/successpath

Chapter 10:

Networking and Collaboration

Cultivating Connections for Musical Growth and Financial

Gains

For the dad who understands the power of connections, this chapter delves into the world of networking and collaboration within the music industry. Discover how building relationships can not only elevate your musical journey but also lead to lucrative opportunities.

The Role of Networking

In a music industry driven by relationships, networking is a cornerstone for success. A survey by Music Business Worldwide found that 75% of industry professionals consider networking crucial to their career advancement. For dads looking to monetize their musical passion, cultivating a strong network can open doors to paid gigs, collaborations, and more!

Musical Collaborations: Strength in Numbers

Collaborations are more than just creative endeavors; they're business opportunities. Teaming up with other musicians, producers, and artists can introduce your music to new audiences. A joint effort combines your strengths and talents, creating a synergy that resonates with listeners.

Cross-Promotions and Features

Collaborating with fellow musicians can extend beyond creating music together. Cross-promotions, where you feature each other's work on your respective platforms, amplify your reach. A study by Nielsen Music found that fans of featured artists are more likely to listen to the song, leading to increased exposure and potential income.

Leveraging Industry Events

Industry events like music festivals, conferences, and workshops offer invaluable networking opportunities. According to Pollstar, the global concert industry generated over $10.4 billion in revenue in 2019. Participating in such events not only exposes you to industry professionals but also potential collaborators and clients.

Online Communities and Social Media

The digital era has expanded networking opportunities to online spaces. Platforms like LinkedIn, Facebook groups, and music forums allow you to connect with professionals and fellow musicians globally. Utilize these spaces to share your expertise, engage with peers, and foster meaningful connections.

Pitching Your Expertise

Networking isn't just about receiving; it's also about giving. Showcase your musical expertise by contributing articles, tutorials, or insights to music publications, blogs, and podcasts. This positions you as a knowledgeable figure within the industry, attracting opportunities for paid collaborations and speaking engagements.

Nurturing Long-Term Relationships

Networking isn't a one-time activity; it's about building genuine, lasting relationships. Maintain regular communication with your network, offer support, and celebrate each other's successes. According to a study by Harvard Business Review, 65% of new business comes from referrals from existing clients and contacts.

Monetizing Collaborative Ventures

Collaborations and networking can lead to various monetization avenues. From joint concerts to revenue-sharing on streaming platforms, the financial opportunities resulting from these connections can be diverse. A study by MIDiA Research found that artist-to-artist collaborations boosted streaming revenues by 30% in 2020.

A Melody of Connections and Earnings

Networking and collaboration are more than strategies; they're investments in your musical journey. By fostering connections with fellow musicians, producers, and industry professionals, you're not only expanding your musical horizons but also creating pathways to financial growth!

In summary, as you navigate the world of networking and collaboration, remember that every interaction you cultivate has the potential to shape your musical trajectory. Whether you're co-writing songs, partnering on projects, or participating in industry events, the world of connections invites you to orchestrate a harmonious blend of musical growth and financial gains!

Ready to turn your passion into reality?
Follow the link and begin your journey!

www.rock-dads.com/successpath

Chapter 11:

Marketing and Branding

Strategies to Amplify Your Musical Brand and Income

For the dad seeking to turn their musical passion into a thriving business, this chapter explores the dynamic realm of marketing and branding. Discover how strategic promotion and a strong musical brand can not only boost your reach but also lead to increased income.

The Power of Effective Marketing

In a crowded digital landscape, effective marketing is the key to standing out. A study by the Content Marketing Institute revealed that 90% of successful marketers prioritize their audience's informational needs. For dads aiming to monetize their musical passion, understanding your audience and crafting a compelling message is essential.

Defining Your Musical Brand

Your musical brand is more than just your music; it's the essence of what you represent. Define your unique style, values, and mission. A consistent and authentic brand creates a memorable identity that resonates with fans and potential clients.

You can not spend too much time at the beginning of your journey on defining your brand. Your brand and your story are the cornerstones of your business and how you indirectly engage with your audience. When they see you or your brand, it needs to be clear and concise what solution you are providing and to whom.

Crafting a Professional Online Presence

Your online presence is often the first impression you make. Create a professional website that showcases your music, services, and portfolio. According to a study by Blue Corona, 38% of visitors will stop engaging with a website if the content/layout is unattractive.

There are numerous web services out there that have templated sites or allow you to customize your own within their system. It doesn't have to be overly complicated, but it is the face of your brand and should look professional and easy to navigate for an optimal experience for your potential clients.

Leveraging Social Media Platforms

Social media is a powerful tool for reaching your audience and building a loyal following. Platforms like Instagram, Facebook, and Twitter provide avenues to share your music, engage with fans, and promote your services. A study by Sprout Social found that 74% of consumers follow brands on social media for entertainment.

The fact that it's basically free advertising for your brand and music doesn't hurt, either. If you have followers, you have a warm audience. That warm audience is more likely to engage with, purchase from, and recommend your brand. This is where consistent engagement with content is key.

Content Marketing: Sharing Your Expertise

Content marketing involves sharing valuable insights and knowledge related to your musical expertise. Blog posts, videos, and tutorials not only establish you as an authority but also attract an audience seeking your guidance. A report by Demand Metric indicated that content marketing generates three times more leads than traditional marketing.

Most of this content can be repurposed as well. There are AI services now that will take a long-form piece of content that you made, say a podcast or livestream, and automatically break it down into smaller, consumable parts that can then be used to seed your social sites. Doing this helps with content creation and consistency!

Email Marketing and Fan Engagement

Building an email list allows you to communicate directly with your fans. Send out regular newsletters featuring updates, exclusive content, and special offers. According to Statista, the click-through rate for emails in the music and audio industry was 3.47% in 2020.

Your website and how you are driving traffic is critical to building out your list. Having a subscribe button and a way to collect user data that you will use to send them information is a very strong way to keep your audience engaged with the brand.

Showcasing Client Success Stories

If you're offering musical services like teaching or production, showcasing client success stories will build credibility. Testimonials and case studies illustrate the impact of your expertise. A study by BrightLocal found that 85% of consumers trust online reviews as much as personal recommendations.

When someone else can attest to your methodology or skillset, it gives more credibility to everything you say after. That builds trust and confidence that your product or service is the right solution for them. You may not be able to showcase testimonials at the beginning of your entrepreneurial journey, but do not forget this piece once you have the opportunity to collect. Their value is immeasurable.

Paid Advertising and Targeting

Paid advertising on platforms like Google Ads and social media can amplify your reach. Utilize targeting options to reach specific demographics interested in your musical offerings. A study by WordStream found that the average click-through rate for Google Ads in the music industry is around 2.69%.

The prospect of starting an ad campaign can be scary, but it's really easy once you've played around in their system. And you don't have to spend a ton of money to start. Set a budget for a couple of bucks per day to send people to your website, watch the dashboard for whatever service you're running your ad, look for that approximately 2-2.5% click-through rate, and make adjustments from there. If you are below 2%, there are different things you can do to determine what to fix to improve, but it will be dependent on your specific situation. It's nothing to be scared of since there is plenty of information out there, and the service you use should offer client support.

Monetizing Through Strategic Marketing

Effective marketing isn't just about gaining attention; it's about converting interest into income. By strategically promoting your music, services, and brand, you're not only expanding your audience but also paving the way for increased earnings!

In summary, as you navigate the world of marketing and branding, remember that each promotional effort is an investment in your musical venture. Whether you're engaging with fans on social media, sharing your expertise through content, or leveraging paid advertising, the world of marketing invites you to compose a symphony of success that harmonizes your passion and profit!

Ready to turn your passion into reality?
Follow the link and begin your journey!

www.rock-dads.com/successpath

Conclusion:

Transforming Passion into Profit

Embrace Your Musical Journey with Confidence and Purpose

Congratulations, fellow music-loving dads, on embarking on a journey to monetize your passion for music! Throughout this guide, we've explored a symphony of strategies that can transform your love for melodies into a source of income, all while staying true to your musical aspirations. As we draw the final curtain, let's reflect on the key harmonies that have resonated through these chapters!

A World of Opportunities

From teaching music lessons and creating original compositions to live performances and music production, we've uncovered a myriad of ways you can channel your musical talents into profitable ventures. According to a study by PwC, the global music industry revenue is projected to reach $131 billion by 2030, underscoring the wealth of opportunities awaiting those who harmonize their passion with strategy.

The Power of Adaptation

The music industry is dynamic, with trends and technologies constantly evolving. By embracing digital distribution, streaming platforms, virtual performances, and emerging tech tools, you position yourself to thrive in this ever-changing landscape. According to a study by Deloitte, music streaming revenues are predicted to grow by 25.5% annually through 2025.

Diverse Income Streams: A Melodic Ensemble

We've explored how diversifying your income streams, whether through merchandise, music licensing, wellness sessions, or tech innovations, can create a wealth of financial stability. As reported by the Bureau of Labor Statistics, the median annual wage for musicians and singers was $30.39 per hour in 2020, showcasing the potential for profitable musical pursuits.

Connecting Through Collaboration

Networking, collaborations, and building a resonant musical brand aren't just industry buzzwords; they're the cornerstones of your success. By nurturing connections, partnering with fellow musicians, and engaging in meaningful collaborations, you're tapping into a global community that appreciates and values your musical contributions.

The Melody of Marketing and Branding

Crafting an authentic musical brand and effectively promoting your talents can amplify your reach and earnings. As the Content Marketing Institute highlights, effective content marketing can increase your website's conversion rates by six times, illustrating the power of strategic messaging and engagement.

The Path Ahead: Notes of Encouragement

As you venture forth, remember that each note you play, every song you compose, and every connection you make contributes to your musical journey. Monetizing your passion for music isn't just about finances; it's about harmonizing your love for melodies with the fulfillment of sharing them with the world!

So, dear dads, seize the stage, embrace the studio, and explore every avenue that resonates with your musical soul.

Whether you're teaching a student, creating a composition, or sharing your melodies online, your musical journey is a tapestry of creativity and purpose. Embrace the rhythm of your passion and the melody of your dreams, and let your musical journey continue to crescendo into a symphony of success!

Ready to turn your passion into reality?
Follow the link and begin your journey!

www.rock-dads.com/successpath

Appendix:

Resources for the Musical Entrepreneur

Tools, Platforms, and Organizations to Support Your Journey

Having access to the right tools, platforms, and organizations can be a valuable asset. This appendix compiles a list of resources that you can use to inform your musical journey and guide you toward achieving your goals. From music education to marketing assistance, this collection, though not exhaustive, is designed to support you every step of the way.

1. Online Learning Platforms:

- Udemy: Offers a variety of music-related courses, from music theory to production techniques.
- Coursera: Provides online courses from universities and institutions on music business, composition, and more.

2. Music Distribution and Streaming Platforms:

- DistroKid: Enables you to distribute your music to various streaming platforms and keep 100% of your earnings.
- TuneCore: Offers distribution, publishing, and licensing services for independent musicians.

3. Music Licensing and Sync Opportunities:

- Songtradr: Connects musicians with opportunities to license their music for film, TV, ads, and more.
- Artlist: Provides a platform for licensing music for video projects.

4. Virtual Event Platforms:

- StageIt: Allows you to host paid live-streaming concerts and interact with fans in real-time.
- Eventbrite: Enables you to create and promote virtual music events and sell tickets.

5. Music Production Software and Tools:

- Ableton Live: A popular digital audio workstation for music production and live performances.
- Logic Pro: A versatile DAW for Mac users with powerful music creation and editing capabilities.

6. Music Marketing and Promotion:

- Hootsuite: A social media management platform to schedule and track your social media posts.
- Canva: A design tool to create eye-catching graphics for your music promotions.

7. Music Associations and Organizations:

- American Association of Independent Music (A2IM): Supports independent music labels and artists.
- Music Business Association (Music Biz): Provides resources and networking opportunities for music industry professionals.

8. Music Industry News and Insights:

- Billboard: Offers news, charts, and insights into the music industry's trends and developments.
- Hypebot: A blog that covers the latest news and strategies for independent musicians.

9. Legal and Copyright Information:

- **U.S. Copyright Office**: Provides information on copyright registration and protection for your music.
- **LegalZoom**: Offers legal advice and services for musicians, including contract templates.

10. Networking and Collaboration Platforms:

- **LinkedIn**: A professional networking platform to connect with fellow musicians and industry professionals.
- **SoundBetter**: A platform to find music production professionals for collaborations and projects.

11. Music Performance Rights Organizations (PROs):

- **BMI (Broadcast Music, Inc.)**: Collects royalties for public performances of music compositions.
- **ASCAP (American Society of Composers, Authors, and Publishers)**: Represents and protects the rights of music creators.

12. Music Industry Conferences and Events:

- SXSW: An annual conference and festival that covers music, film, and interactive media.
- Midem: An international music business event that focuses on networking and innovation.

These resources serve as stepping stones on your path to monetizing your passion for music. Explore, experiment, and take advantage of the opportunities that resonate with your goals and musical aspirations. Remember, your journey is unique, and these tools are here to support you in creating your symphony of success!

Ready to turn your passion into reality?
Follow the link and begin your journey!

www.rock-dads.com/successpath

Author's Note

I'm a dad of two and a stepdad to one. I never really thought that in my lifetime, I would be able to say either of those statements. I'm eternally grateful for the opportunity and the responsibility of being a dad…it also scares the hell out of me!! Until I became a stepdad to an amazing young girl, I didn't think that fatherhood was a page in the book of my life. Since then…and two children of my own…the weight of being a parent has always been present, and I never really felt up to the task in a way that I was going to leave a legacy for my children. Because of a health scare I had in early 2022, I decided I needed to change things.

None of us are promised tomorrow, and the time you squander today is the time you wish you had back on your deathbed. As morose as that may sound, the truth can not be denied. You only have so much time, and what you do with it affects not only you but also everyone you care about and are responsible for. You have a chance—and dare I say an obligation—to leave a legacy, and I believe that legacy should be rooted in what you are most passionate about. This humble ebook is an attempt to help you find the starting point of your legacy and the fervent hope that you will follow through. The first step is always the hardest, but with support and the adamant desire to change the trajectory of your life, you can truly change the world.

If you are ready to begin, follow the link to www.rock-dads.com/successpath to get **90%** off a 15-day course to start monetizing your passion for music! This is the same blueprint that I used to begin my own journey (and I *didn't* get this deal)!

Keep rockin' dads! 🤘

Matt

Like, share, follow, and join Rock Dads!!

Online: www.rock-dads.com

Facebook: www.facebook.com/groups/rockdads

YouTube: www.youtube.com/@rockdads

TikTok: www.tiktok.com/@rockdads

Instagram: www.instagram.com/rock.dads/

Discord: www.discord.gg/rockdads